Cinderella Burning

Ameena Mayer

While every precaution has been taken in the preparation of this book, the publisher assumes no responsibility for errors or omissions, or for damages resulting from the use of the information contained herein.

CINDERELLA BURNING

First edition. September 24, 2023.

Copyright © 2023 Ameena Mayer.

ISBN: 979-8223094272

Written by Ameena Mayer.

To the fire within us.

Cinderella Burning

I toss ice cubes
into my head
to put out the fire

they klink
against my skull
as if in a glass of gin
for once, I can't hear
the empty room

before they melt
please eat pancakes
with me at the diner
the one with the good memories

we'll zigzag
to the hot pink booth
listen to "comfortably numb"
on the jukebox

we'll twirl across the crusty floor
laugh at the empty room
until the Elvis clock strikes midnight

before thoughts defrost
flames ignite
and I turn to ash

can I at least have this?

Memory of Colours

let me wake up in marmalade
a sweet, sticky baptism
into the lighter religions

throw that clowning sun at me
like a yellow carnation
let me catch it as a bridesmaid
scorched from anticipating love

place fuchsia in my footsteps
embarrassing the old-school grey
of pavement, an endless face furrowed
in cracks of disapproval

let me slide brightly
across emerald dance floors of grass
past the tick-tock box filled with black
to the fair ride running up the sky
with the freedom of children
make me swing across sapphire jewels of air
like a queen's lullaby

may the hours pass like champagne bottles
exploding their golden bliss
onto the stiff white sheet of time
let me sleep drunk on the memory of colours
never to wake again

The Last Creator

She tried, oh, she tried
to dance for the hard faces of dimes
like a starved ballerina for a numb audience.

"My free market system,"
That One said, "it's gonna eat you up
with its teeth sharpened on my coins.
Your blood will spill like Kool-Aid.
Your bones will break like chalk.

She felt splattered
against That One's steel tongue.

"Your free market system,"
she yelled, "it's not gonna eat me,
'cause I grow things deep inside.
I've got trees shooting roots through my veins,
love curled in the crimson caves
of my thumping heart,
a green idea and songs and recipes.
I create, so ain't no chipped tooth gonna chomp me."

"You sure are brave," That One hissed,
"but I promise
you will slave over jobs
sweat to keep your house
struggle to raise your children

and my free market system will suck it all away
with its black hole mouths
will suck you out
light from a star
leaving nothing but a quiet scream."

"I'll tell you what I'll do," she cried,
tears slapping cheeks
like the hands of That One's words
but eyes straight ahead
spine strong, arms spread.
"I'm gonna eat your free market system
with its ugly teeth and crazy mouths
and from deep inside
my stomach's gonna change it,
gonna soften and stretch and smooth it.
Then I'll spit it into Earth's warm womb."

She did.
And smiles and daisies
dragonflies and carrots
porcupines and kisses
dances and rivers
grasses and laughter
bluebells and birthday cakes
sprang from the soil.

"I create," she said, shining like Venus.
"Ain't no one gonna suck me out."

That One, eyes down
spine hunched, hands clenched

walked away
with a quiet scream.

The Chill

now days of amber light
trickling over pavement like rum
shaking frigid city strides into dance
have passed

no longer do sun's maternal hands
rub bronze on skin
her warmth has receded
like tide from shore, leaving dried white twigs,
crumbled sand stroked relentlessly
by thick, demanding fingers of wind

now air cuts sky like frosted glass
sun drops too easily in mimic of leaves falling
like broken dreams that rested soothed
in heated days of laughter, wine, music

pinks, yellows, blues no longer
wrapping bodies like cotton candy
the somber procession of greys and blacks
shift slowly against darkening horizon
as the chill taps spines, old skeleton hand of fall
pushing us inside to burrow and long
for something absent

can we have one last escape
into alarming warmth

AMEENA MAYER

one final traipse
into sunlit spaces shielding minds
from the cruel clutch of thought?
can we have one more day of brilliance?

Torn Moth Wings

so much laughter once
frothing, delinquent rivers
now silence sits between us
like buckets of ice

under gold sheets of sunlight
sifted through half-open blinds,
I clutched in dripping fistfuls
your warm mango flesh
now iron in the straight armchair

touching you,
a dream faint
as the torn moth wing
by rain-punched window
through which I can barely see
our happiness,
green mountain trees
behind globs of mist

Where Are You?

where are you? I can't decipher you
from the robotic grey blah

among cars hurling themselves
like bombs down streets
Gap ads for gaudy sweatshop tanks
spider legs scuttling
across nine-to-five clocks
the collage of Starbucks coffee cups
I can't see you, can't hear you anymore

we used to play in fields
flooded with forget-me-nots
the chirps of robins falling like petals
as we sat with sandwiches and smiles
sharing ideas about the way the world curves

now you send me emails every so often
thin, mute "how are you's" gleam
like contorted black insect parts on snow
I never know how to respond
how to find you in all that cyberspace

where are you? I can't feel you anymore
the computers and cell phones
have shredded our roots
we're not meant to be imprisoned

in small concrete rooms
with only the drone of TV,
blue light grazing us
like a careless lover

between the careers and trophies
I can't sense you anymore
we used to rely on each other for survival
live in one camp
tell stories under stars
the crackling fire warming us
we used to know each other from birth to death
our smells and sounds and songs
splash through lakes held in summer's palm
rock each other within the grey grip of winter

now "how are you" stains the screen
cuts into me like tight thread
if I respond, "fine, but where are you?"
you'll never know what I mean

Why I Left You (in clichés, since everything between us was so typical)

I strolled through the garden
in a pink satin nightgown
moonlight dripped from the sky
drenched me with longing
a balmy breeze enveloped me
in its soft arms

a skeleton stood by a rose bush
its bones shone like ivory silk
a slit of silver lit up its eye sockets
like tinsel

it reminded me of beauty

I inched towards it as it plucked a red rose
extended it to me gracefully
its elegant bones smelling of sandalwood

as I reached for the rose
the silver in its sockets
expanded like wind-kissed flames
my heart fluttered, an uncaged bird
yearning for something
I thought I lacked

"Will you love me?" it said,
its voice a cobra coiling around me
I stepped back, chuckling, and said,
"I already have, a million times,"
then strolled away
dreaming of something new

Galaxy Girl

as I walk downtown
coats roughly brush by
until I'm tilted like a dissonant song
unheard by the human eye

in the line-up to the movies
a man caresses a woman's face
like a genie's bottle
his wishes stuffed inside her like gold
my lead cheeks are smacked by cold
his tenderness confuses me

I don't belong here
among bars bloated with noise
cafés bursting with chattering bodies
dreaming of disco lights

my slim, silent steps take me home
the trees fade as shadows
of what I've missed
streetlamps bend over me
inspect me like I'm an alien

at least the houses look warm;
through their windows, fat pillows of light
spill into the dark
but the people inside are strangers

and I've lived here all my life

I look up, search for hope
the night sky is a sparkling womb
devouring me, and I see:
I belong to the starlight
the supernovas, the suns
only in their shining heat
and explosions can I exist

I know no one
and no one knows me
only the arms of the galaxy
embrace me

The Smart Seashell

do not ask me to achieve.

let me be
just a seashell
plain white and beige
filled with gentle air
singing naturally within myself
the peace of hollowness
teasing barnacled rock
soaked ropes of rolling seaweed

let me sit smoothly in the rough sand
i'll gorge on fat drops of sunlight
without shame
and ignore the hectic children
carving out empires
by the violent chill
of shaking sea

The Whales Inside Me

plastic lodged in the belly of a whale
retched onto shore
the screech of seagulls
scratch its rotting carcass

once a queen with polished silver flesh
robed in salt water and sun
gliding through her kingdom
of elegant waves

what Martian pain invaded
after she ate Safeway bags
holding coke and chips,
our apathy churning
in the gut of royalty?

and I recall your words,
garbage bags bloated with antique rot,
your shaking fists spoon-feeding them to me
as if they were peas or ice cream
I gobbled them passively
not knowing the difference between this
and "I love you"

years later they slump in my stomach
on cold yellow days
they twist like sick whales

Letter to a Lost Friend

Dear lost friend:

Our run together was christened with fat noodles
at the cheap diner on Cambie Street.
We traded stories of childhood trauma.
Caught up in an idea, you accidentally
tossed your chopsticks over your shoulder.
We laughed.

Seven-year soul sisters
like two seashells echoing the wind the same way.

You taught me guitar. We were committed
to emo rock, Radiohead the soundtrack
crashing through our days.

Platters of veggie sushi.
Strolls, bandana-strewn, down Commercial Drive.
Tofu samosas in Grandview Park.
Beer and garlic fries at Subeez Café.
Stomping around in circles at the beach
naked behind curtains of night
warm with homemade fruit wine
ranting about men, the war,
how people are too judgmental about bodies.

(Remember the time

we drank Grower's peach cider
at Beaver Lake in Victoria and a police boat
pulled up right in front of us?
Poker-faced you, we got away with it
and you took a picture of the boat
so we could joke about it later.)

Your smile was kind, like a ballad.

Gorgeous musician, but more and more,
crouched on my bed chipping reeds
for your bassoon while I sprawled patiently
beneath stones falling from your mouth,
gasped quietly on the moonscapes of your moods.

Tom Yorke's wails starkly naked without the racket of us,
I left his CDs in my mother's home.

But I still have your homemade cards
with masterful drawings from the cartoon "Cow and Chicken,"
Cow clutching her bright pink udders,
expostulating through flying tears,
thin, droopy Chicken trying to calm her down.

(No, I lied. I threw them out a few years ago during a midlife crisis.)

I don't know when I became the broken ride
in your fair of boys and gigs and concerts and boys,
but you said friends and family were no longer for you,
a boulder flattening my bones even now.
Candles no longer in your eyes, just ash.

You stopped calling me, took on the look
of a distant relative I had known in some happy childhood.

I don't know why years later, I still Google you,
why I wish you'd think of me, as if that would fill
the empty tunnels, make it all okay.

With confusion,

Your Ex Soul Sister

P.S. I didn't want this to be for you.
I wanted to write about the leaves, the pipelines, my cat.

Erotic Rainbows

the river runs through my memories of you
they're soft and gentle like you

the sun crashes to the ground
there's no one around
but your moonlit eyes pull me in
and I've never been
so . . .

your star-spun hair
your ocean-full stare
your wisdom lives in trees
your songs fill a thousand seas
and I'm saved

when the air is grey
and my soul walks away
velvet visions of you
pull me through
and I'm saved

(erotic rainbows fumble and soar
lipstick-smeared kisses fall to the floor
honeydew patches, nebulous green
fire-struck gazes in gasoline)

the river runs through my memories of you

they're soft and gentle like you

Since You Left

your hands were warm
they opened towards me
like grand oak doors
spilling sunlight on my flesh
showing me glimpses of sky

when they closed
blackness smothered me
like shot ravens
that not even God can lift.

your eyes were glowing wormholes
that pulled me through blazing tunnels
of twirling planets, crackling suns

since they've closed
I've been stuck on a moon
half-formed and frozen
in a pocket of space
that not even God can find.

your body reeked of lightning
jolting my heart into dance
resurrecting me into a Frankenstein
whose beauty only you could feel

but you left

now everyone runs from me
when they hear my cries

even God.

Twelve-Hour Lover

Twelve-hour lover, you have chiseled the scabs
incised by the question of my worth.
I should've gone home, left your mouth gaping for more,
hooked fish on land, but your plush lips
pushed out the dry, stone part of me,
my oyster pearl of holding in
leaving moist, messy depressions
needing to be filled.

When our limbs entwined like seaweed
and I clutched your jellyfish skin,
I fell into an oceanic trench
crouched there like an archaic, spiny fish
wanting to hide in your darkness forever
in this knowing that you want me, spines and all
that I'm not curled in a cold ball
waiting for the phone to ring.

Too soon, it's over, your back facing me,
Great Wall of China
across which all the wars play themselves out
blood draped in curtains blotting the sunshine.

For hours I lie wide-awake
drowning in waves of black sheets
wishing for the love to come back.

In the morning, it lasts five minutes.

Then the shower, the house tour, the quiet ride home.
Saltwater stings my wounds.
As you drive off, sea floors of distance spread between us
and I know I won't see you again.
Even if I do, it's only because you want to be a gentleman.

Now your face thrusts through my mind like a knife.
I'm a gutted fish impaled on its spines.

Past Despair

when the day grows old
the night unfolds
and dreams are frozen and grey
I'll take you there
to the indigo air
where the trees haven't faded away

I'll take you there
past the knot of despair
where the raven and eagle soar
where the eye grows calm
with the coming of the dawn
and the Somalian boy cries no more

we build and burn
past the point of no return
we pleasure our bodies
without much concern
for the fingers that bleed
the wars that proceed
the bellies and babies that yearn

I'll take you there
past the knot of despair
where the raven and eagle soar
where the eye grows calm
with the coming of the dawn

and the Yemeni girl cries no more

beyond the dead road
there's a sunset and sea
that can hold all our dreams
if you take my hand
you'll understand
what peace and loveliness mean

I'll take you there
past the knot of despair
where the eagle and raven soar
where the eye grows calm
to the coming of the dawn
and the Haitian girl cries no more
and the Ukrainian boy cries no more
and the Afghani girl cries no more
and there are no tears no more

True Morality

Be lazy.
This is the only moral path.

beyond cars scuttling
like ravenous rats
sprawl on the beach
watch the sky roll
like a movie screen
until your heart slows
like a lover's hand
let oceans of sunlight
drown the impulse
to be frantic

unravel the bun
undress the foot
let in the wind
run past concrete
dive into silent woods
sink into soil
until it occupies you
and you're colonized by moss

dunk your unsheathed legs
like swords in a lake
until you own its peace
impale the convulsing beast

of doing

Prayer to End Chronic Pain

tug me from my body like string
tie me to the wind
let me glide as a kite
defying the hand that holds it

so tired of this broken body
weighed down by bricks
some giant tossed in a rage
now I wait for rescue
a wrecked car in a ditch
by a long, abandoned road

let me shock flocks of geese
with my lightness and speed
released from steel wires in my leaden flesh
(I'm still waiting for the tow truck)

hang me from the sun
with its infinite pirouettes
let me rise, set, rise, set
in floods of orange and red
warmer than the blood
sticking to my bothered veins
like stale jam
(won't someone offer me
a sandwich while I wait?)

expand me beyond all memory
of useless bones and tissue
remembering only the sky

Dinosaurs (in memory of the Indian Ocean tsunami, 2004)

the tsunami came, grey dinosaur
shredding skin as if it were Kleenex
rolling vibrant colours of life
into thick, wet balls hurled back to sea
leaving emptiness as wide
as a child's screaming mouth

strange, I think, this grisly collage
of destruction, disease, faces twisted with pain
smeared across screens and papers:
their uncanny resemblance
to dead Sudanese villages, refugee camps
creaking off baked desertscapes
I saw not long ago

the only difference:
the raucous clink of coins
from G8 governments
the richies with the Midas complex
sweeping survivors away like dust
thrusting resorts like nails
into the blistering wounds
of their homeland

only a bunch of hopeless victims
who can't offer us much

except what's left of their soil,
they say
(except their very selves, I think,
if anyone cared to notice
the raw humanity in their eyes)

besides, the world says, that crisis
is as old as prehistory
and we've no more interest
in the footprints of dinosaurs

Dream Lovers

Two stars collide
like ice skaters on frozen lake
the explosion melts ice
shatters darkness.

The moon is a bright white pearl
pinned to the coat of night
like you to my heart
illuminating my caves
old desires for union.

We open wine bottles
like ore to find gold
drink until arteries tingle
as we entwine, green garden snakes,
stretching in innocent beds
of First Grass.

We swim through rainbows,
giddy scuba divers in psychedelic sea,
until the breeze lifts us higher
and we are lovers in an angel's hand
warmed by a harmless sun.

Now Pegasus steals us
we clasp its silver mane as we kiss
racing through cotton wool clouds

gliding across blue carpets of sky
the primordial whoosh of wings
matching the thump of our hearts
that shed dust and shimmer
like electricity.

We soar through tsunamis
unscathed by the crash
onto craggy shore
we twirl through tornadoes
unharmed as we bash
into fridges and cars
insulated by the thick foam of love
grown only from a desperate willingness
the struggle of salmon upstream
the bloom of lightning-struck tree
the single fiery flower
in the snow.

Boxes

Work Box:
the military buzz of fluorescent bulbs
shakes smiles off faces
commands shoot out like bullets
papers litter desks like corpses
hands clutch glowing coins
mistaking them for stars
only black holes here
sucking laughter from suits
that droop in trenches
wishing for peace
the glide of one sunbeam
through the blinded window

Home Box:
she shivers under
the frosty glare of TV
solitary fork slumps in plate
whose magenta flowers
mock the hard edges of her routine
(shower, eat, sleep, clean)
a cruel Santa has stuffed her in this box
wrapped in grey wallpaper
she's a discarded Christmas present
waiting to be opened

Invisible Boxes:

disabled, depressive-disordered
marginalized, mediocre
she bleeds inside these prisons
screams for circles, zigzags,
one democratic line
leading to freedom
from glaring eyes,
measuring tape
that shove her away
from the flight of seagulls
the rise of sun
after the darkest night

Trickery of Shadows

sun splatters black paintings onto pavement
they lead her as she hobbles down the road
caress her crinkled skin, her trampled soul
with silent promises

in one of these works of light
she sees a young girl, broad-shouldered and tall
wearing a black gossamer dress
a wreath of scorched roses in her hair

the girl floats through metal poles
like a dark angel
glides under stomping feet
unharmed

then evening's cold hand
brushes the woman's watery eyes
the paintings grow faint
and die

Another Prayer to End Chronic Pain

I want hurricanes to twirl through me
eat up relentless cobwebs
swaying from bones
spun by some manic spider
its legs sprawled in my belly
like iron fingers

let me flow from my body,
lava from volcano,
cool under the soothing moon
like a smooth lake in winter

I need to gobble giant stars
that supernova the ache out
infuse pale blood with rainbows
arteries tripping on the wild beat
of psychedelic heart

help me throw off this albatross skin
let me sit like a peeled banana
sweet, unsullied as a virgin
before the first bite

On Missing Dad

why did you try so hard
to teach me ice-skating?
were you preparing me
for when your death
would cut across my cold
soul like a blade?
the pattern of scars reminds me
of the chess boards we used to play on
pawns falling down
predicting the tumble
of your truck into ditch.
some omnipotent hand
flung you off the face of the earth
like old laundry, now you hang
off frozen branches of universe.
I can't grab you, fold you up
place you safe in my drawer
wear you to school
to lonesome walks by the sea
we used to swim in.

remember the bitter oysters you fed me?
I had to drown them in catsup
as I do now to memories of you.
you said oysters are full of zinc
I sometimes think
you are an element now

the oxygen I breathe in
or aloe plants breathe out
like the ones you rubbed
on my scraped knees.
I wish I could smear some across
my slitted heart.

remember when we used to run together?
I just won third place in the track race
recalled your graceful lopes.
when you died, the wind heard
your strong long bones
snap like twigs.
on gusty autumn days
when dead leaves crash to the ground
dry and broken
the sound harasses my ears.

I've pushed the tears behind my eyes
there's an ocean in my head
sometimes it smashes hard against skull
reminds me that I miss you.

The Loneliest Night

I cling to my cat like a buoy
in the stormy sea of my bed
the rumble of cars fizzles out
like stale soda
the evening sky is a stranger
misunderstanding me

where are all my tortured friends
patchouli drenched
crunching my cornflakes
ironing musty shirts
on my antique piano bench
repeating stories of narcissistic lovers
to dissident strums of guitar?

who didn't notice my unshaven leg
sagging bra strap, the worn-out dishcloth
whom I could crawl into
like an old velvet chaise
not trying to touch stars

now as the judging moon
glares through the window
like sterilized tin
I voyage alone
through oceans of blankets
my face plunged deep

in the warmth of black fur
like my whole life is there

Season of Longing

jaws of autumn
munch warm chunks of summer
like lemon cake

now fog rises like hung laundry
concrete stones mark the death of trees
I'm incised by the chilled edge of memories
friends that fled from my branches
to chase the fading stain
of wings on horizon

left with my skeleton's twist
under sun's pale yellow eye
that peers through the bulging lens
of wind-warped sky

wishing for winter's anonymous white
to cover me like a mother's shawl
sing me lullabies of shimmering snowflakes
anaesthetize the longing
to be cocooned in praising green
the bells of birds returned
the generous arms of spring

Forget Us

you plan your diamond first-world futures
our broken limbs buried beneath the ore
oh, your white houses stand so high
scrape the sun from our skies
you sweep our frozen bodies under doormats
with thoughtless brooms

your bombs blast soft brown bodies
filling your car tanks, our carcasses
are in the trunk, but don't open it
forget us

while you work, spend, work, spend
with plastic cards that cut our veins
our crimson blood falls like hot rain
stains your designer umbrellas

but don't look up, look down at the concrete
a gravestone for your ancient forests
decaying beneath with the murdered ancestors
of Indigenous Peoples

while you strive for New Age perfection
in your party balloon lives
don't watch as they pop in our faces
leave scars as deep as dry riverbeds

as you build, burn, build, burn
get more keys and keys and keys
McDonald's coke cell phone cellophane
don't see our tired hands aching in every item
our futures are lost but don't look for them
forget us

while you surf the net for pop-culture styrofoam
disregard the waves carrying our screams
don't think we deserve to be
on this planet as equals as you bend crookedly
with reverence beneath your flags
blowing in the ferocious wind of our howls
pierce velvet coats with poppies
in remembrance of you who died in wars
forget us

we break, bleed, toil
for your glass towers, jets, corporate jobs
forget us

we are in your air, water, soil, blood
we are your brothers, sisters, mothers, lovers
we are the song in your veins
without which you will die
but forget us
forget us.

Just Another Poem about Christmas

mandarin orange sting
drunken Baileys bang
tease of rainbow lights
pot of gold chocolate lies

party invite paranoia
family reunion hysteria
stale champagne
bubbles popped
in chipped Santa mug

child born but lost
in hollow carol drawl
church malls jingle
the lost miracle

candied coin poison
blood red gift wrap crackle
tree genocide elegy
strangling bows, box traps
homeless man's
Halloween melody

Christmas card flurry
empty lines on white
bird tracks on new snow
the only joy

When the Sky Falls

the wind yelled like an angry man
the sky shattered on me, robin blue china,
and sank through my skin

the wounds were deep
I tugged miles of cloud from them
in light white garlands
redecorated branches of air
like it was Christmas

crows and geese
burst from my chest,
candy from piñata,
screeching for heaven
celebrating release

I felt I had given birth
and at least for a moment
I couldn't hear the tornadoes
of words shaking my insides
from all the people who nearly hated
but not enough to ignore

the sky had to splinter
to remember wholeness

as I wrenched the sun

from my singed heart
held it solemnly in burning hands
I knew this would heal

Winter Murder

snowflakes fall like phantoms
on broken tree limbs, bleeding stump
smothering sticky sap wounds

amber and white mingle
life and death
love and war

all these old, cracked stories told here
where chains slice bronze freedom
under the distant stare of winter sun

Bravery of a Daisy

your screams
blow off my petals
they shiver on the grass
like abandoned children

I become a circle of stamen
yellow and coarse like an old thumb
pushing naked with longing
into the dark, thick chest of dusk

the sky stiffens as a frozen lake
at my protrusion
then thaws for golden bouquets
of voluptuous stars
blooming in the sky
healthy
perfumed with fire

I feel ashamed
why did I let you do this?
even the moon gleaming like a silver dime
won't grant me a spotlight

but my show isn't finished
though I can never be loved
bald and alone
I stand straight to greet the dawn

Ode to Leaves

leaves, you sway like a lullaby
on hammocks of breeze
sing your green song through me
so I dream of your image

oh leaves, do your hard veins
carry smooth, green blood
that runs fast like rivers
when butterflies kiss you?

leaves are soft decorations
making hard, wrinkled trees
feel human, feminine, young again
leaves are wigs hiding trees' baldness
from glaring sun

autumn leaves bring sunlight
from sky to ground
the soil is on fire with orange and red flames
we must rake them up
before we burn
with too much passion

leaves have fallen
grass glitters with gold and copper
who said money doesn't grow on trees?

cruel wind, don't snatch leaves away
trees scratch sky with frantic, nude limbs
the gorgeous brown flesh of soil shivers
she yearns for leaves to cover her
like a lover

the tree must be dying
for the leaf is crying
tears of sap
it knows are flying
bright and sweet
from the swinging axe

leaf, you're a cruel deathbed
rocking ladybug to sleep
who is dreaming of gentle, green things
oblivious of spider approaching

leaves drip dew drops
like my tongue wet for sweetness
reflections of green
tremble in each crystal orb
predictions of freshness
drenched life to come

leaves fly like birds through sky
with no destination
aimless leaves, like my crumbled mind
do you want to drown in the river
to be carried to infinity?

Homesick for Outer Space

I yearn to leave the dirty, thick confines
of Earth's atmosphere
plunge into clean, weightless space
uncut by grudging borders of nations
electric lines, the crisscross of concrete
I want the unadulterated health of space
without the stench of fuel suffocating Earth
like a pillow held over a baby
by the cruel hands of humans

I just want impersonal, emotionless black
with only the faint smell of fire and metal
illuminated by a stationary sun
not rising and setting, pacing from east to west
as if looking for a lost mate
amongst the ruin and strain below

inside a planet's atmosphere, reality is blurred
we think our wars, creations, agony, elation
are all there is
but space holds the permanence of nothingness
the truest, easiest reality
punctured by ancient orbs of rock and gas
forged by the imagination of pure love

I need the peace of space
not needing to be saved

Don't miss out!

Visit the website below and you can sign up to receive emails whenever Ameena Mayer publishes a new book. There's no charge and no obligation.

https://books2read.com/r/B-A-HHVV-KFVNC

Connecting independent readers to independent writers.

Also by Ameena Mayer

Love from an Alien Sun
Cinderella Burning

Watch for more at https://linktr.ee/ameenamayer.

About the Author

Ameena Mayer has a Masters in English Literature and is a college English teacher in Vancouver, British Columbia. She has always believed that the written word has the power to heal and create positive change. When she isn't writing poems and novels, she enjoys singing covers of classic rock songs and dreaming of a better world. She hopes you have the chance to hug a tree today.

Read more at https://linktr.ee/ameenamayer.